When all seems lost
        the salty sea too deep
we find
        fins or feet
on this revolving home we share
        no matter where
sea or air
        the faithful tide
                family.

—AA

THE Spirit of SPRINGER

THE REAL-LIFE RESCUE OF AN ORPHANED ORCA

AMANDA ABLER

Illustrated by
LEVI HASTINGS

little bigfoot
an imprint of sasquatch books
seattle, wa

Cool fog hung above the salty depths of the Puget Sound, engulfing a ferryboat that would soon rumble away from Vashon Island to downtown Seattle.

Swoosh! A smooth, round head broke the glassy surface.

In the water bobbed a lone baby orca.

A ferry worker on board was surprised
to see the orca by herself.

A resident orca spends its entire life
in the same pod swimming
close to its mother.

Where was her
mother now?

The ferry worker phoned a friend, an experienced whale watcher who was in close contact with orca researchers. Within a day, whale experts came to visit the little orca. They were worried.

Who was she? Where was her family?

The scientists listened to the calls and whistles the orca made.

She didn't sound like the orcas from the pods that make up the J clan and often swim near Seattle.

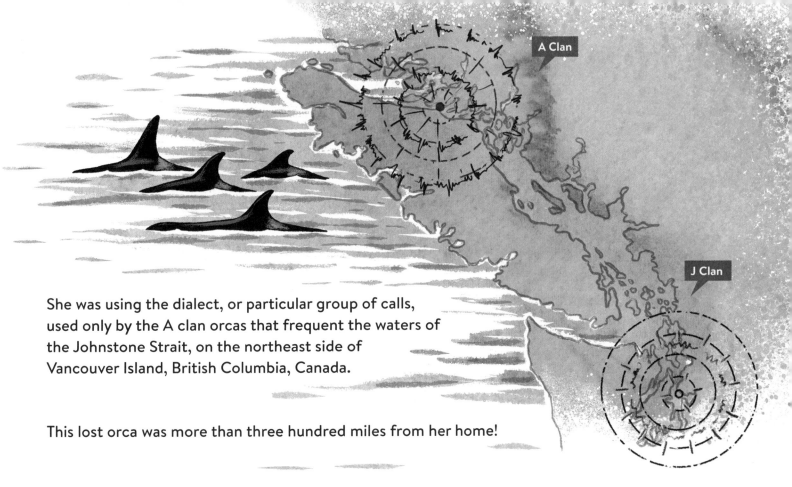

She was using the dialect, or particular group of calls, used only by the A clan orcas that frequent the waters of the Johnstone Strait, on the northeast side of Vancouver Island, British Columbia, Canada.

This lost orca was more than three hundred miles from her home!

The scientists looked through pictures of orcas from the different pods that make up the A clan. They matched the orca's white eye patch to one in the pictures. The mystery orca was two-year-old Springer (A73)!

No one had seen Springer's mother in more than a year.
Everyone assumed Springer was now an orphan.

But Springer still needed a mother. She was lonely.

She rubbed up against the ferries, trying to snuggle.

She loved when people visited her. She would roll on her back to let them rub her belly.

She needed love and attention just as much as she needed food.

VISITING DAY: FEBRUARY 2002

Word of Springer traveled quickly to Dr. David Huff, a veterinarian at the Vancouver Aquarium. He and Dr. Lance Barrett-Lennard, a marine mammal scientist who also worked there, felt a responsibility for this little orca who had wandered away from their country.

They decided to visit her.

Motoring out from Seattle in a little boat, they didn't take long to find Springer.

Dr. Dave gave Springer a checkup. Her skin was covered in sores.

Lance noticed she had horrible breath! The spray from her blowhole smelled like nail polish remover. This was a sign that Springer was starving.

They knew Springer couldn't survive much longer on her own. They wrote a letter to the US agency that is responsible for protecting marine wildlife, urging them to try to reunite Springer with her family in the Johnstone Strait.

DECISION TIME: MARCH 2002

The agency wondered what to do. No orca had ever been captured and successfully released back into the ocean.

Many people following Springer's story worried that if she were captured she would end up in an aquarium. No one wanted that life for Springer.

Lost and lonely, Springer began swimming in a small area and playing for hours all by herself with her favorite stick.

She was running out of time. If the agency wanted to reunite her with her pod before they migrated north for the winter, she needed to return to the Johnstone Strait by the end of the summer.

After much public debate and input from the scientific community, the agency decided to try to rescue Springer and nurse her back to health. Once she was strong enough, they would return her to the Johnstone Strait.

Clear skies stretched above calm seas as Dr. Dave and the rescue team headed out to find Springer. Lance didn't join them, as he had returned to Canada eager to prepare for Springer's return.

Nosy news helicopters thumped loudly overhead. The team found Springer in her usual spot where they had visited and played with her every day for a month to gain her trust.

Dr. Dave watched nervously from a boat nearby. The team rubbed and scratched Springer's back as they attempted to slip a rope loop around her tail so she wouldn't be able to dive away. Over and over they tried without luck.

Then suddenly the rope was around her tail! Dr. Dave couldn't believe it had worked. Divers quickly jumped into the water to hold Springer upright, so she could breathe, and pulled a sling under her body.

A crane lifted her out of the water onto a foam pad on a barge, where the team immediately began spraying her with ice-cold water.

Springer headed for a water pen in Manchester, Washington, just an hour away.

Here she would stay until she was strong enough to make the much longer trip back to Canada.

Springer also needed a full checkup before she would be allowed to return home to be sure she didn't have any disease that she might pass on to her family.

Meanwhile in Canada, Lance was as busy as a curious octopus working with his team to set up a second water pen close to the Johnstone Strait, where they would await Springer's homecoming. Years earlier, he had fallen in love with orcas while being a lighthouse keeper. Now he was an expert on orcas and on patience.

Springer seemed comfortable in her water pen in Manchester, Washington. However, Dr. Dave didn't want her to like the pen or people too much. She might not want to leave, or she might seek people's attention once she was released.

The scientists and aquarium workers cared for Springer around the clock. They hid behind screens and used a remote-controlled camera to watch her. They knew how lonely she was and how much she wanted love and attention. They were heartbroken to not play with her.

Springer needed to remember how to catch food once she was back in the wild, so the scientists fed her live salmon through a pipe that emptied into her pen.

At first, Springer barely ate. Why wasn't she hungry?

Dr. Dave noticed worms in her poop. He gave her medicine to kill the worms, and soon she was gobbling up every salmon that popped out of the pipe.

Even though Springer was eating well, Dr. Dave still needed to heal her skin. Springer was enjoying playing with her favorite stick so much that the crew gave her more logs and sticks to rub on.

That did the trick! The logs rubbed off Springer's old skin, like a washcloth in a bath. The sores on Springer's skin began to heal.

Finally, Dr. Dave was ready to check Springer for diseases. The American scientists ran tests on her blood. The Canadian scientists ran the same tests. At last everyone agreed: Springer was healthy enough to go home!

MOVING DAY: JULY 13, 2002

The rising sun painted the sky red as Dr. Dave and the team prepared Springer for her voyage home. A bald eagle, a symbol of strength for many First Nation peoples, circled overhead. This was a good sign for little Springer, who would need plenty of courage for this next part of her journey.

Divers slipped a sling around Springer, and a crane lifted her into a tank filled with ice-cooled water on a boat. Soon they were skimming across the water toward the Johnstone Strait.

In late afternoon, they arrived at Dong Chong Bay in Canada, just outside the strait, where Lance and his crew were waiting for her, ready to take over her care. However, Lance's team wasn't the only one there to welcome Springer.

The rhythmic beat of drums filled the bay as a group of First Nations people paddling canoes and watching from the cliff-lined shore greeted Springer. A 'Namgis chief welcomed Springer in both his Kwak'wala language and English.

The air buzzed with excitement as a crane lifted Springer out of the boat and placed her onto a foam pad atop a barge waiting at the mouth of the bay.

As the barge puttered into the cove, a lone eagle swooped down from high above, joining the gathering.

The barge reached the new water pen and the crane lifted Springer up again. As Springer hovered in the air, a second eagle appeared. The two birds circled aloft, silently overseeing the event.

Then, just as Springer touched down into the water, the eagles broke their silence, seeming to cry out in welcome.

Lance and Dr. Dave blinked back tears. They had not expected such an outpouring of love and spirit for the little orca on this special day.

Come midnight, under a clear sky sprinkled with stars, most everyone was ready for sleep. Except Springer.

Full of energy, she breached and slapped her tail as she explored and chased salmon in her new pen.

She was happy to be home!

Lance reluctantly left Springer and headed to bed. Just as he was climbing into his sleeping bag, he heard distant orca calls over the hydrophone, an underwater microphone he and the team were using to listen for orcas.

A pod of orcas was approaching the bay. Lance's heart raced. Could this be Springer's family?

For a moment, Springer fell silent. This was the first time she had heard another orca calling in her dialect in over a year. She was so excited she could only make nonsense whale sounds, just like someone might scream, "Ahhhh!" when surprised at a birthday party.

She breached and squealed, pushing at the net as she tried to get out.

Eventually, she calmed down enough to call normally to the other orcas.

Lance jumped up and grabbed a headset to listen more closely. One of the scientists confirmed the pod was an A pod, containing Springer's relatives.

Should we release Springer? Lance wondered. He was afraid she would break through the net on her own. But she wasn't wearing her tracking sensors yet, and it would be impossible to follow her in the dark. Unsure he was making the right choice, Lance decided to wait.

Early in the morning, the pod swam away. As the orcas' calls faded into the distance, Springer settled down as well.

RELEASE DAY: JULY 14, 2002

After a few hours of sleep, Lance was up again along with Dr. Dave and the rest of Springer's team. The A pod from the previous night had been spotted swimming around the nearby islands.

As the pod began swimming toward Dong Chong Bay, Lance realized this might be the right time to release Springer. The crew hurried to ready her with tracking sensors.

In the afternoon, the pod swam past the mouth of Dong Chong Bay, but then suddenly turned back and entered the bay. The pod was swimming straight toward Springer's pen!

Springer squealed and wiggled all over.

Lance was shocked! Was this the right moment to let her go?

Dr. Dave had no doubts. This perfect opportunity was more than he had hoped for.

The team members around the bay radioed back and forth and took a quick vote. They cared deeply for Springer and felt so much responsibility for her. Everyone agreed; it was time to release Springer. They may never have a better chance to reunite her with her family.

The divers in Springer's pen released the net and she sprinted off,
a free spirit at last!

Cheers and applause erupted across the bay as she bolted for the pod.

This was the moment everyone had worked so hard for.

But then, halfway out to the pod, Springer was distracted by a kelp bed, the orca version of a playground. As she frolicked in the seaweed, the team waited anxiously, then breathed a sigh of relief as Springer resumed swimming toward the orcas.

She approached and stopped just short
of the pod.

Lance held his breath as Springer and
the other orcas hung motionless in the
water, staring at each other.

Then . . .

The pod turned and swam slowly away, and Springer swam in the opposite direction.

Lance's heart sank. Springer was free, but would she reconnect with her family?

Later that evening and through the next day, Lance followed Springer's location using her tracking sensors. She was trailing the pod. This was a good sign. Lance knew she wanted to be part of her family again.

Dr. Dave reluctantly returned to his work at the Vancouver Aquarium; with Springer freed, he knew his job on this project was complete. Now he would have to rely on Lance to share any news about Springer.

Over the next few days, Springer was spotted swimming with several different pods, but she always ended up alone.

Lonely and needing love from her family, Springer even tried to befriend a boat.

In the early morning, Lance and a fellow scientist set out in their boat yet again to look for Springer.

They received word over the radio that a large gathering of orcas, a superpod, had been spotted nearby. Could Springer be part of this group?

By the time they arrived at the superpod, the group was just breaking up. Through binoculars and falling mist, Lance scanned the orcas for Springer.

The last group to leave the superpod was one of the A pods.

The other scientist with Lance counted the orcas; there was one extra calf swimming next to a female named Nodales, Springer's cousin. The calf swam toward them. It was Springer!

Nodales followed Springer and pushed her back toward the pod. "Silly Springer," Nodales seemed to say, "boats aren't toys!"

Relief washed over Lance. He had worried how they would teach Springer to stay away from people and boats. Now it looked like the other orcas would do the job for them. For the first time, Lance was truly hopeful that Springer would find an adoptive mother. He couldn't wait to share the news with Dr. Dave.

Lance returned to the Vancouver Aquarium, joining Dr. Dave. The animals there needed them more than Springer now, but she was always on their minds.

Over the next few months they received reports that Springer was spotted with Nodales and another female named Nahwitti.

In the fall, she left the Johnstone Strait area with Nahwitti and orcas from two different A pods, likely traveling north for the winter.

Winter blew into the Pacific Northwest, cold and wet, and the rainy months trickled by. The scientists wondered and worried about Springer. Was she being fully accepted into her family? Would she still be with the pods when they returned to the Johnstone Strait? Only time would tell.

In February 2003, a group of thirty orcas swam into the waters of the Queen Charlotte Strait, just north of the Johnstone Strait. The incoming report said that Nodales was with them, but to Dr. Dave and Lance's disappointment, not Springer.

As spring bloomed into summer, more orcas returned to the Johnstone Strait area, but there was still no sign of Springer.

Then, on July 9, 2003, nearly one year after her release, Springer swam through the Queen Charlotte Strait with Nahwitti and Nahwitti's mother, Yakat.

Springer had fattened up over the winter. How happy and healthy she looked to have found a family at last!

Springer's rescue and release was a success. Everyone was elated. She had touched so many hearts.

Lance marveled at the orcas' strong sense of community, amazed that the pod had welcomed Springer back.

For Dr. Dave, Springer would forever remain his most special patient and her release his greatest success story.

FAMILY TIME: AUGUST 2016

The sun sparkles off the waters of the Queen Charlotte Strait. Every year since Springer's release, Lance has been here, watching and waiting patiently for Springer to return from her winter migration with her pod.

Through binoculars, Lance spots Springer and Nahwitti swimming in unison. Between them a third, smaller dorsal fin appears. The orca calf bounces between Nahwitti and Springer, her mother.

Lance snaps a picture of the family and smiles.

Springer's rescue has brought not just one life, but two to this pod. She found a mother and became one as well.

As Springer turns and swims away,

beside her trails her baby named Spirit.

SOLVING A MYSTERY

The Spirit of Springer is a true story about a mystery orca calf found swimming alone in the Puget Sound. The little orca was spotted by several people in the area before she settled into her favorite spot, hanging around the Vashon Island ferries. The story focuses on the experiences of Dr. Lance Barrett-Lennard, a marine mammal scientist at the Vancouver Aquarium, and Dr. David Huff, a now-retired veterinarian, also from the Vancouver Aquarium. However, the real rescue mission of Springer involved the effort of many caring people, government officials, and scientists, including the National Oceanic and Atmospheric Administration (NOAA) in the US and the Department of Fisheries and Oceans (DFO) in Canada.

Once the little orca appeared, solving the mystery of her identity was top priority. Eventually, Springer was identified through photo matching, voice recognition, and DNA testing. This was the first of many steps toward reuniting Springer with her family in Canada.

PHOTO MATCHING: Whale scientists keep track of who is who in the orca community by taking pictures of the orcas and noting differences in their markings and dorsal fin shapes. Graeme Ellis, a longtime whale researcher who worked at the Pacific Biological Station in Nanaimo, British Columbia, matched the white eye patch of the mystery orca to a photo of Springer's white eye patch.

Springer (A73), enjoying Chinook salmon

VOICE RECOGNITION: Helena Symonds, a whale researcher who works at the OrcaLab in British Columbia, listened carefully to a recording of the little calf's calls. She immediately recognized a unique call that she had heard only from Sutlej, an orca from the A pods that often swim off the coast of Vancouver. Because orca mothers pass their calls on to their calves, Helena knew at once that the calf must be Sutlej's baby, Springer!

DNA TESTING: A skin sample was taken from the mystery calf so that her DNA could be analyzed. By comparing the results to a DNA database of orcas that Dr. Lance Barrett-Lennard had developed, he concluded that the calf was Springer.

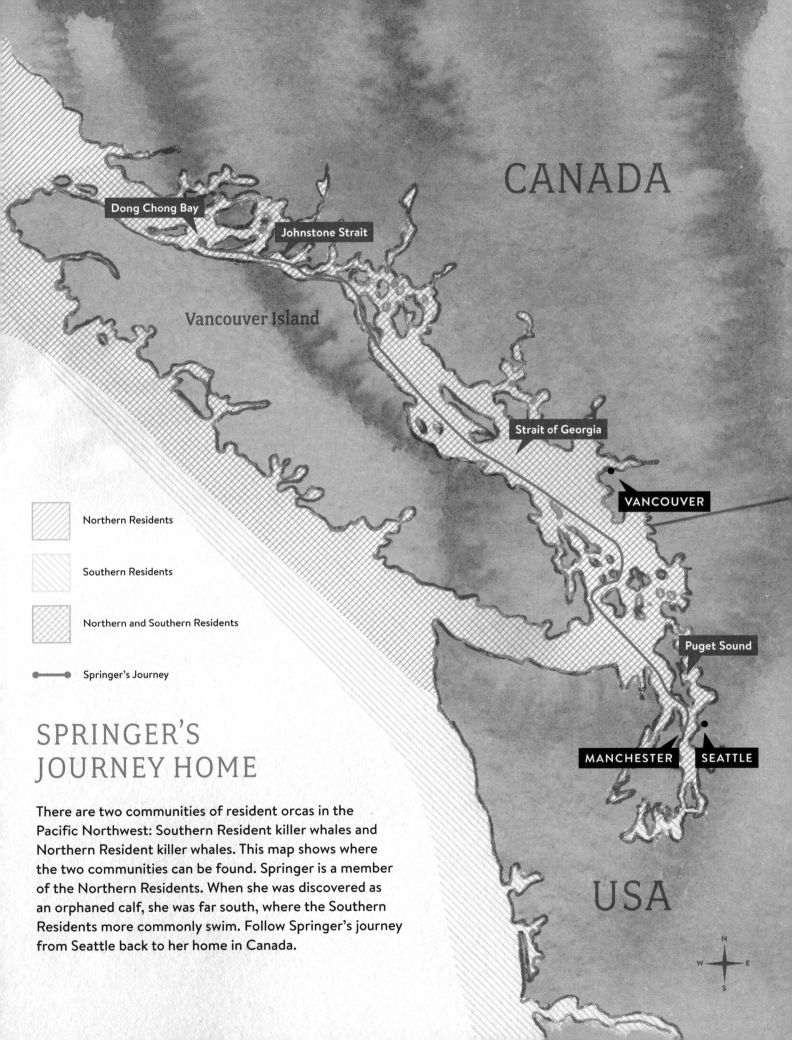

CANADA

Dong Chong Bay

Johnstone Strait

Vancouver Island

Strait of Georgia

VANCOUVER

Puget Sound

MANCHESTER   SEATTLE

Northern Residents

Southern Residents

Northern and Southern Residents

Springer's Journey

SPRINGER'S JOURNEY HOME

There are two communities of resident orcas in the Pacific Northwest: Southern Resident killer whales and Northern Resident killer whales. This map shows where the two communities can be found. Springer is a member of the Northern Residents. When she was discovered as an orphaned calf, she was far south, where the Southern Residents more commonly swim. Follow Springer's journey from Seattle back to her home in Canada.

USA

WHO IS SPRINGER'S FAMILY?

Orcas swim in groups called *pods*. Scientists give each orca a number that corresponds to its birth order within the pod. Springer is also known as A73, because she is the seventy-third orca born into the A pods. All the A pods make up the A clan like one big extended family.

Resident orcas, like Springer, live in matrilineal (mother-led) pods, meaning that every orca in a pod is the offspring of a female within that pod. Before Springer was orphaned, she always swam with her mother, Sutlej (A45); her grandmother,

Kelsey (A24); and other members of the pod. Later, Springer was adopted by Yakat (A11) and her daughter Nahwitti (A56). They were all born into the A4 pod.

Nodales was a member of the A5 pod. Scientists don't know exactly how Nodales and Springer were related. However, they do know they were family because of the similar calls they shared, indicating that they were both part of the A clan.

There are many other members of the A clan that are not shown in this family tree.

A CLAN

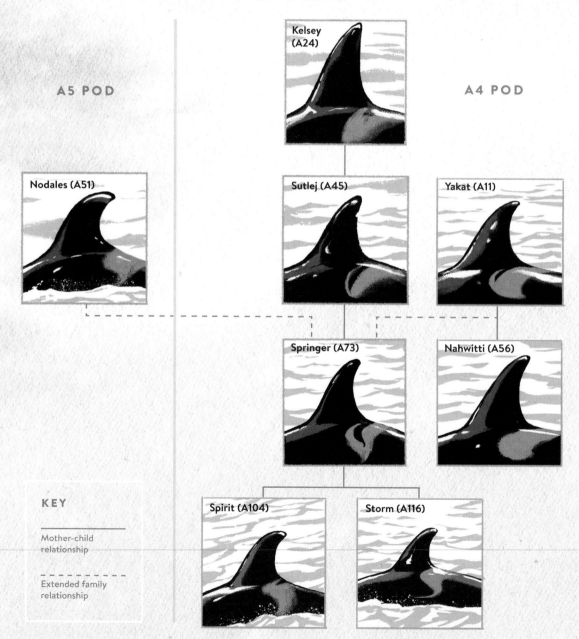

A5 POD

Nodales (A51)

A4 POD

Kelsey (A24)

Sutlej (A45)

Yakat (A11)

Springer (A73)

Nahwitti (A56)

Spirit (A104)

Storm (A116)

KEY

Mother–child relationship

Extended family relationship

ANOTHER BABY FOR SPRINGER

In 2017, Springer gave birth to another orca calf, named Storm. Little Storm can be seen swimming next to Springer in the photo below. Although Spirit, Springer's first calf, is not in this photo, she normally swims alongside Springer and Storm as well.

PACIFIC NORTHWEST ORCA FACTS

SCIENTIFIC NAME: *Orcinus orca*

COMMON NAME: Orca, killer whale. Scientists usually use the term *killer whale*. In recent years, the term *orca* has become more popular with the general public, most likely because it avoids using the word *killer*. Both names are considered correct.

Nevertheless, orcas are not actually whales, but instead are a type of dolphin.

LENGTH: 16 to 26 feet. Males tend to be longer than females.

WEIGHT: 1½ to 6 tons

TOOTH LENGTH: 3 to 4 inches

TYPES OF ORCAS: There are three different types of orcas that live in the Pacific Northwest: resident, transient, and offshore. The three populations live separate lives and rarely interact with each other.

Springer is a resident orca. Like other residents, she swims close to shore and eats mostly Chinook salmon. Transient orcas roam coastal waters and eat marine mammals such as seals, sea lions, and sometimes small whales. Offshore orcas swim farther out to sea and eat fish and sharks.

ORCA COMMUNICATION: Because light travels poorly in water and sound carries easily, an orca's primary sense is hearing, not sight. An orca's call can swiftly travel many miles underwater. Orcas use sound to communicate with each other and to "see" underwater by using echolocation, a process of emitting clicks and creating an image based on the way the sound echoes back to the orca. Orcas can even use echolocation to "see" inside each other's bodies.

A team member who was in the water pen with Springer helping with her care said she could feel Springer's calls and clicks in her chest, the way someone might feel the musical bass from a car's radio when the volume is turned up loud.

SPRINGER STILL AT RISK

The lives of Springer and all orcas in the ocean are at risk. Local government agencies list the dwindling Southern Residents as endangered and Northern Residents as threatened. Boat collisions are a serious threat. Many resident orcas can't find enough salmon to eat because of overfishing and dams that block salmon from reproducing. Sound pollution from ships, sonar scans by the Navy, and explosives used in underwater drilling for oil can damage an orca's hearing, making it difficult to echolocate and muffling their calls.

Pollutants in the oceans also pose a serious threat to orcas, especially to little ones like Springer's calves, Spirit and Storm. Toxic chemicals wash down streams and into the oceans where they are absorbed by tiny fish and plankton. Small fish eat these little creatures, which are then eaten by salmon, passing along more and more toxins. The orcas at the top of the food chain receive large amounts of these poisons when they eat salmon. The toxins are then passed on to nursing calves through their mother's milk.

WHAT CAN YOU DO TO HELP SPRINGER AND HER FAMILY?

1. Properly throw out all trash, recycle, and compost whenever possible to cut back on trash in landfills.

2. Encourage your family to avoid using fertilizers and pesticides in your yard.

3. Try to buy organic food to reduce the amount of pesticides washed into the ocean.

4. Talk to your parents about using less-toxic household cleaners. Do a quick search on the web to find out how to make your own cleaners from common household items.

5. Organize trash cleanups in your neighborhood and keep trash out of storm drains.

6. Avoid visiting theme parks that keep captive orcas or dolphins. Visiting these places encourages the capture of more dolphins and orcas, further reducing the population in the wild.

WHERE CAN YOU SEE ORCAS?

If you live in or visit the Pacific Northwest, you can go on a whale watch to see the orcas in person. To find where whales may often be viewed from land, visit TheWhaleTrail.org.

If you live far from orcas, you can see them live through cameras placed in the Johnstone Strait by OrcaLab. Click on the Orca Live link on OrcaLab.org and maybe you will see Springer swim by!

DIVING DEEPER

Check out these resources to explore more about Springer and other orcas!

BOOKS

Operation Orca: Springer, Luna and the Struggle to Save West Coast Killer Whales by Daniel Francis and Gil Hewlett. Madeira Park, BC: Harbour Publishing, 2007.

Scientists in the Field: The Orca Scientists by Kim Perez Valice and Andy Comins. Boston: Houghton Mifflin Harcourt Books for Young Readers, 2018.

A DOCUMENTARY ABOUT SPRINGER'S RESCUE

Orphan Orca: Saving Springer, National Oceanic and Atmospheric Administration (NOAA), 2005. Available on YouTube.

WEBSITES

Center for Whale Research
WhaleResearch.com

Fisheries and Oceans Canada
DFO-MPO.gc.ca

NOAA
NOAA.gov

OrcaLab
OrcaLab.org

The Whale Trail
TheWhaleTrail.org

Wild Killer Whale Adoption Program
KillerWhale.org

Wild Whales
WildWhales.org

To anyone who has lost their mother —AA

To my grandmothers, who always encouraged the aquatic
obsessions of a landlocked farm boy —LH

Manufactured in China by C&C Offset Printing Co. Ltd.
Shenzhen, Guangdong Province, in December 2019

LITTLE BIGFOOT with colophon is a registered trademark
of Penguin Random House LLC

24 23 22 21 20   9 8 7 6 5 4 3 2 1

Editors: Christy Cox and Ben Clanton | Production editor: Jill Saginario
Designer: Tony Ong | Photography by Lynne Barre, NOAA Fisheries (page 42);
Lisa Spaven, Fisheries and Oceans Canada (page 45)

Library of Congress Cataloging-in-Publication Data

Names: Abler, Amanda, author. | Hastings, Levi, illustrator.
Title: The spirit of Springer / Amanda Abler ; illustrated by Levi Hastings.
Description: Seattle, WA : Sasquatch Books, [2020] | Audience: Age 7. |
Audience: K to grade 3. | Includes bibliographical references and index.
Identifiers: LCCN 2019015998 | ISBN 9781632172129 (hard cover : alk.paper)
Subjects: LCSH: Killer whale--British Columbia--Juvenile literature. | Killer
whale--Washington (State)--Juvenile literature. | Animal rescue--British
Columbia--Juvenile literature. | Animal rescue--Washington
(State)--Juvenile literature. | Wildlife reintroduction--British
Columbia--Juvenile literature. | Wildlife reintroduction--Washington
(State)--Juvenile literature. | Puget Sound (Wash.)--Juvenile literature.
| Johnstone Strait (B.C.)--Juvenile literature.
Classification: LCC QL737.C432 A25 2020 | DDC 599.53/6--dc23
LC record available at https://lccn.loc.gov/2019015998

ISBN: 978-1-63217-212-9

Sasquatch Books
1904 Third Avenue, Suite 710
Seattle, WA 98101

SasquatchBooks.com

AMANDA ABLER grew up in New Hampshire where she developed a love of snow, being on the water, and maple syrup. Pursuing her interest in science, she earned a BS in biology from Massachusetts Institute of Technology. She loves writing nonfiction because of all the interesting things she gets to learn and the new people she gets to meet. Amanda lives in Seattle with her family and their small, ferocious dog, Bear. *The Spirit of Springer* is her authorial debut.

LEVI HASTINGS is an illustrator and cartoonist based in Seattle. His work reflects his lifelong obsessions with natural science, travel, history, and queer culture. He's been published in a wide range of outlets, from regional papers like the *Stranger* to national periodicals like the *Washington Post Magazine.* You can find more about him on his website, LeviHastings.com.